Looking at Animals on PLAINS and PRAIRIES

To Jack
With love from
playgroup xx.

First published in Great Britain in 1999 by

Belitha Press Limited,
London House, Great Eastern Wharf,
Parkgate Road, London SW11 4NQ

This paperback edition first published in 2000

Copyright © Belitha Press Limited 1999
Text copyright © Moira Butterfield 1999

Series Editor Honor Head
Series Designer Hayley Cove
Picture Researcher Juliet Duff
Map Artwork Robin Carter / Wildlife Art Agency
Animal Symbols Arlene Adams

All rights reserved. No part of this book may be reproduced or utilized in any form or by any means, electronic or mechanical, including photocopying, recording or by any information storage and retrieval system, without permission in writing from the publisher, except by a reviewer who may quote brief passages in a review.

ISBN 1 84138 161 6 (paperback)
ISBN 1 84138 020 2 (hardback)

Printed in China

10 9 8 7 6 5 4 3 2 1

British Library Cataloguing in Publication Data
for this book is available from the British Library

Photographic credits
Frank Lane Picture Agency: 9, 12, 18, 25, 26 David Hosking, 10 E&D Hosking. NHPA: 11 Christophe Ratier, 19 Daryl Balfour, 20 John Shaw, 22 Anthony Bannister. Oxford Scientific Films: 6 Frank Schneidermeyer, 8 Daniel J Cox, 13 Stan Osolinsk, 21 Michael Fogden, 23 Patti Murray, 27 Jen & Des Bartlett, 29 Wendy Shattil and Bob Rozinski. Planet Earth Pictures: 7 Roger de la Harpe, 14 K&K Ammann, 15 Frank Krahmer, 17 Steve Bloom, 24 William S Paton, 28 Adam Jones.
Tony Stone Images: 16 Art Wolfe.
Cover
Oxford Scientific Films: top left Daniel J Cox.
Frank Lane Picture Agency: top right David Hosking.
Planet Earth Pictures: bottom Roger de la Harpe.

Looking at Animals on PLAINS and PRAIRIES

Moira Butterfield

Belitha Press

Introduction

Plains and prairies are large open spaces where there is plenty of grass but not many trees. Most plains and prairies are hot places, but a few are cold.

Animals that eat only plants live here because there is plenty of food for them to munch. They are called herbivores.

Hunting animals live here because there is lots of food for them to catch and kill. Animals that eat meat are called carnivores.

Contents

- Lion 6
- Zebra 8
- Gazelle 10
- Vulture 12
- Elephant 14
- Cheetah 16
- Giraffe 18
- Termite 20
- Aardvark 22
- Agama lizard . . . 24
- Ostrich 26
- Prairie dog 28

Where they live 30

Index of words to learn . 32

Lion

African lions sleep a lot during the day when it is hot. They are predators and prowl around at night when it is cool, looking for other animals to chase and kill.

A family of lions is called a pride and baby lions are called cubs. A male lion has long hair called a mane.

Zebra

Zebras live in big groups called herds. They move around the plains of southern Africa looking for grass to eat and water to drink. They all have stripy coats but each animal has its own special pattern of stripes which is different from all the other zebras.

Gazelle

Gazelles live in herds on the African plains. Lots of hunting animals like to eat them. While they move around eating grass they listen for enemies.

If they hear a noise they sniff the air to find out if their enemies are nearby. If they need to, gazelles can run fast to escape.

Vulture

Vultures are scavengers. This means they do not hunt animals. Instead they find dead ones to eat. They can see a long way and they can smell very well too. They spread their big wings and glide high in the sky, looking down below for food to eat.

Elephant

The African elephant is the largest animal living on land. It needs a lot of food and it spends all day looking for grass and leaves to eat.

Baby elephants live with their mother and their aunts. If a lion comes too near the biggest elephants chase it away.

Cheetah

The cheetah is a big cat that lives on the flat plains of Africa. It is a fierce hunter, with sharp claws and teeth. Cheetahs catch and eat other animals. They are the fastest animals in the world. A cheetah can run as fast as a speeding car and much faster than a person.

Giraffe

Giraffes are good at reaching up to pull leaves off the tallest trees. Drinking is more difficult because they have to reach a long way down to the water.

While a giraffe is busy drinking it is in great danger because a crocodile could swim up and grab it.

Termite

Termites are tiny plant-eating insects
that live in big groups called colonies.
Each colony works together to build
a mud nest that looks like a giant tower.
Inside there are lots of secret tunnels
where the insects can hide away
from the hot sun.

Aardvark

The aardvark loves to eat termites. It has strong claws for ripping holes in termite nests and an extra-long tongue for licking out the insects.

The aardvark digs a burrow to hide in during the heat of the day. It closes its nostrils while it is digging to keep out dust.

Agama lizard

Little agama lizards live in groups on the African plains. They spend their days hunting for insects or resting in the sun. When an agama lizard is scared or angry its skin changes colour from brown to bright blue or orange.

Ostrich

The ostrich is the largest bird in the world. It lives on the African plains where there are lots of plants and insects for it to eat. It cannot fly but it can run very fast.

It has strong legs and kicks hard if it is attacked. Ostrich eggs are very big, about the size of a football.

Prairie dog

Prairie dogs are not real dogs. They live in big underground burrows with lots of tunnels and special places for storing food and looking after babies. A burrow also has escape tunnels in case the prairie dogs are attacked by enemies or the burrow is flooded by rain.

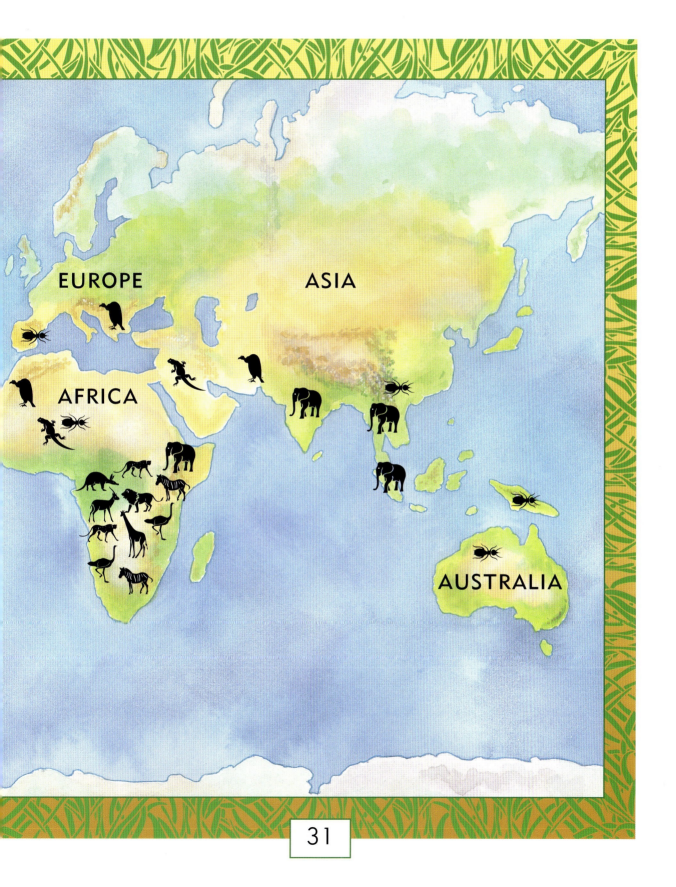

Index of words to learn

burrow an underground home 23, 29

claws sharp, pointed nails for scratching
or grabbing something 17, 23

colony a big group living together 21

herd a big group of larger animals, such
as zebras 9, 11

glide to float through the air with
outspread wings 13

predator an animal that hunts, kills and
eats other animals 7

pride a family of lions 7

scavenger an animal that feeds on dead
creatures it finds 13